PRE-APPRENTICESHIP
MATHS & LITERACY FOR
CONCRETING

Graduated exercises and practice exam

Andrew Spencer

A+ National Pre-apprenticeship Maths & Literacy for Concreting
1st Edition
Andrew Spencer

Publishing editor: Sarah Lang
Project editor: Aynslie Harper
Proofreader: Katharine Day
Text designer: Miranda Costa
Cover designer: Aisling Gallagher
Cover image: Stocksy United/JP DANKO
Permissions researcher: Sian Bradfield
Production controller: Emma Roberts
Typeset by: Q2A Media
Reprint: Katie McCappin

Any URLs contained in this publication were checked for currency during the production process. Note, however, that the publisher cannot vouch for the ongoing currency of URLs.

For product information and technology assistance,
in Australia call **1300 790 853**;
in New Zealand call **0800 449 725**

For permission to use material from this text or product, please email **aust.permissions@cengage.com**

ISBN 978 0 17 047450 4

Cengage Learning Australia
Level 7, 80 Dorcas Street
South Melbourne, Victoria Australia 3205

Cengage Learning New Zealand
Unit 4B Rosedale Office Park
331 Rosedale Road, Albany, North Shore 0632, NZ

For learning solutions, visit **cengage.com.au**

Printed in Australia by Ligare Pty Limited.
1 2 3 4 5 6 7 26 25 24 23 22

A+ National
PRE-APPRENTICESHIP
Maths & Literacy for Concreting

Contents

Introduction

It has always been important to understand, from a teacher's perspective, the nature of the mathematical skills students need for their future, rather than teaching them 'textbook mathematics'. This has been a guiding principle behind the development of the content in this workbook. To teach maths that is *relevant* to students seeking apprenticeships is the best that we can do, to give students an education in the field that they would like to work in.

The content in this resource is aimed at the level that is needed for students to have the best possibility of improving their maths and literacy skills specifically for trades. Students can use this workbook to prepare for an apprenticeship entry assessment, or to even assist with basic numeracy and literacy at the VET/TAFE level. Coupled with the activities on the NelsonNet website, https://www.nelsonnet.com.au/free-resources, these resources have the potential to improve the students' understanding of basic mathematical concepts that can be applied to trades. These resources have been trialled, and they work.

Commonly used trade terms are introduced so that students have a basic understanding of terminology that they will encounter in the workplace environment. Students who can complete this workbook and reach an 80 per cent or higher outcome in all topics will have achieved the goal of this resource. These students will go on to complete work experience, do a VET accredited course, or will be able to gain entry into VET/TAFE or an apprenticeship in the trade of their choice.

The content in this workbook is the first step to bridging the gap between what has been learnt in previous years, and what needs to be remembered and re-learnt for use in trades. Students will significantly benefit from the consolidation of the basic maths and literacy concepts.

Every school has students who want to work with their hands, and not all students want to go to university. The best students want to learn what they don't already know; and if students want to learn, then this book has the potential to give them a good start in life.

This resource has been specifically tailored to prepare students for sitting apprenticeship or VET/TAFE admission tests, and for giving students the basic skills they will need for a career in trade. In many ways, it is a win–win situation, with students enjoying and studying relevant maths for work, and for Trades and Registered Training Officers (RTOs) receiving students who have improved basic maths and literacy skills.

All that is needed from students is patience, hard work, a positive attitude, a belief in themselves that they can do it and a desire to achieve.

About the author

Andrew graduated from SACAE Underdale in 1988 with a Bachelor of Education. In 1989, Andrew went on to attend West Virginia University, where he completed a Master of Science (specialising in teacher education), while lecturing part-time.

In 1993, Andrew moved to NSW and began teaching at Sydney Boys' High, where he taught in a range of subject areas including Mathematics, English, Science, Classics, Physical Education and Technical Studies. His sense of practical mathematics continued to develop with the range of subject areas he taught in.

Andrew moved back to South Australia in 1997 with a diverse knowledge base and an understanding of the importance of using mathematics in different practical subject areas. He began teaching with the De La Salle Brothers in 1997 in South Australia, where he continues to work and teach today. Andrew has worked in collaboration with the SACE Board to help develop resources for mathematics with a practical focus.

In 2011, Andrew was awarded the John Gaffney Mathematics Education Trust Award for valuable contributions to the teaching of Mathematics in South Australia. Andrew received a Recognition of Excellence for outstanding contributions to the teaching profession by CEASA in both 2011 and 2012 and, in 2014, he was one of 12 teachers from across Australia to work in collaboration with the Chief Scientist of Australia to develop a better understanding of the role of mathematics in industry. As part of this role, he undertook research in this area, spent time working with the industry and then fed the results back to the Chief Scientist.

Andrew continues to develop the pre-apprenticeship and vocational titles, based on mathematics and literacy, to assist and support the learning of students who want to follow a vocational career path. He is currently working towards the nineteenth title in this series. The titles have also been adapted in the UK and Asia, as the importance of this type of functional mathematics continues to grow. All schools have students who will follow a vocational pathway and it continues to be a strong focus of Andrew's to support the learning needs of these students.

Author acknowledgements

For Paula, Zach, Katelyn, Mum and Dad.

To the De La Salle Brothers for their selfless work with all students.

To Dr Pauline Carter for her unwavering support of all Mathematics teachers.

To all students who value learning, who are willing to work hard and who have character … and are characters!

LITERACY

Unit 1: Spelling

Read the following passage, and identify and correct the spelling errors.

Comercial concreet is used to build or improove the structural strength of business facilities, such as office buildings, shops, wearhouses or restaraunts. Commercial concrete is used in the floors, or the walls, or even the pavemant outside. Commercial concrete needs to be stronger and more durabel than residential concrete. For this reason, commercial concrete floors often require heavier reinforsement and a more powerful concrete mix.

Commercial concrete floors often experience heavy foot trafic, so they need to be treated with a finish or coating to help prevent stains and genaral wear and tear. They also need to be slip-resistent to prevent patential injuries to employes, customers or anyone who may use the area. If a restaurant has exposed concrete flooring, it is important that the floors are easy to clean from any food or drink spils.

The use of 'tilt-up' concrete walls is becoming a popular option in the constructian of commercial buildings. By using tilt-up concrete walls, buildings can be constructed quickly and eficiently. Tilt-up panels can be bought in a range of diferent shapes and colours. Decoretive precast concrete is used to improve the exturnal appearance of commercial buildings. Some companies will use precast concrete for colums, window sills and wall panels, to add visual interest to the building.

Incorrect words:

_____

_____

Correct words:

_____

_____

Unit 2: Alphabetising

Short-answer questions

Specific instructions to students

- In this unit, you will be able to practise your alphabetising skills.
- Read the activity below and then answer accordingly.

Put the following words into alphabetical order.

Safety boots	Overalls
Hi-vis	Cement
Building plan	Formwork
Aggregate	Agitator truck
Concrete mix	Safety glasses
Wheelbarrow	Batching
Slurry mix	Reinforcement

Answer:

_____

_____

_____

_____

_____

_____

_____

_____

_____

_____

_____

_____

_____

_____

_____

Read the following passage and answer the questions in full sentences.

Brodie and Gordon are thinking about becoming concreters when they leave school. They do some research into the type of work they will be required to do on a daily basis, to help them make their decision. Brodie discovers that concreters are responsible for mixing, laying, compacting and levelling concrete. Once the concrete is level, the concreter is then required to clean and seal the surface. Gordon finds that, as well as learning to mix the concrete with sand, gravel and water, they will need to learn how to pour concrete, using a pump, over steel reinforcement (or 'reo' as it is called on site). Concreters also require basic carpentry skills in order to construct the formwork that they pour the concrete into. The formwork creates a mould for the concrete to ensure that the concrete is set to the right dimensions.

Gordon wants to know what skills he needs to have to work as a concreter. Concreting is a 'hands-on' job that requires practical skills, as well as the ability to solve problems that might arise on site. He finds that he will need a good level of physical fitness to work with concrete, as heavy lifting and manual labour are often required. Gordon has always liked the idea of working outdoors and he feels that he has good basic math skills that can be applied to practical situations. One of Gordon's strengths is that he is safety conscious, which is important to have when working in the construction industry because safety is a very serious matter.

Both Brodie and Gordon understand that they will be spending a lot of time outdoors on building and construction sites, which can often be dirty and noisy. Neither of them are concerned about having to work underground or high above the ground, or having to spend a lot of time on their feet. Brodie is not keen on shiftwork so when he finds out that concreters work regular hours during the week, he thinks that this could be a good career move for him.

Finally, Gordon discovers that he will need to familiarise himself with all of the different materials that go into making different types of concrete. He finds out that the tools he is most likely to use in his daily work are concrete mixers, concrete vibrators, shovels, wheelbarrows, concrete pumps, trowels, hammers and edging tools. Brodie wonders if he will need a special driver's licence to drive a cement mixer or agitator truck and discovers that he might need one if it is required of his job.

QUESTION 1

What tasks do concreters undertake on a daily basis?

_____

_____

QUESTION 2

Why do concreters need to construct formwork?

_____

_____

QUESTION 3

What skills are needed to work as a concreter?

_____

QUESTION 4

What is one of Gordon's strengths and why is this important?

_____

_____

QUESTION 5

What tools will Gordon need to be familiar with, if he becomes a concreter?

_____

_____

9780170474504

MATHEMATICS

Unit 4: General Mathematics

Short-answer questions

Specific instructions to students

- This unit is designed to help you to improve your general mathematical skills.
- Read the following questions and answer all of them in the spaces provided.
- You may not use a calculator.
- You need to show all working.

QUESTION 1

What unit of measurement is used to measure:

a the area to pour concrete?

Answer:

_____

b the compression strength of concrete?

Answer:

_____

c the amount of cement required?

Answer:

_____

_____

d the weight of a sand bag?

Answer:

_____

e the speed of an agitator cement truck?

Answer:

_____

f the length of formwork or boxing?

Answer:

_____

g the cost of a cubic metre of concrete?

Answer:

_____

QUESTION 2

Give examples of how the following might be used in the concreting industry.

a percentages

Answer:

_____

b decimals

Answer:

_____

c fractions

Answer:

_____

d mixed numbers

Answer:

_____

e ratios

Answer:

_____

f angles

Answer:

_____

QUESTION 3

Convert the following units.

a 1.2 metres to cm and mm

Answer:

---

b 4 tonne to kg

Answer:

---

c 260 centimetres to mm

Answer:

---

d 1140 mL to litres

Answer:

---

e 1650 g to kilograms

Answer:

---

f 1.8 kg to grams

Answer:

---

g 3 metres to cm and mm

Answer:

---

h 4.5 L to millilitres

Answer:

QUESTION 4

Write the following in descending order.

0.4   0.04   4.1   40.0   400.00   4.0

Answer:

QUESTION 5

Write the decimal number that is between:

a 0.2 and 0.4

Answer:

---

b 1.8 and 1.9

Answer:

---

c 12.4 and 12.5

Answer:

---

d 28.3 and 28.4

Answer:

---

e 101.5 and 101.7

Answer:

QUESTION 6

Round off the following numbers to two (2) decimal places.

a 12.346

Answer:

---

b 2.251

Answer:

---

c 123.897

Answer:

---

d 688.882

Answer:

---

e 1209.741

Answer:

9780170474504

QUESTION 7

Estimate the following by approximation.

a $1288 \times 19 =$

Answer:

_____

b $201 \times 20 =$

Answer:

_____

c $497 \times 12.2 =$

Answer:

_____

d $1008 \times 10.3 =$

Answer:

_____

e $399 \times 22 =$

Answer:

_____

f $201 - 19 =$

Answer:

_____

g $502 - 61 =$

Answer:

_____

h $1003 - 49 =$

Answer:

_____

i $10001 - 199 =$

Answer:

_____

j $99.99 - 39.8 =$

Answer:

_____

QUESTION 8

What do the following add up to?

a $4, $4.99 and $144.95

Answer:

_____

b   8.75, 6.9 and 12.55

Answer:

_____

c   650 mm, 1800 mm and 2290 mm

Answer:

_____

d   21.3 mm, 119.8 mm and 884.6 mm

Answer:

_____

QUESTION 9

Subtract the following.

a   2338 from 7117

Answer:

_____

b   1786 from 3112

Answer:

_____

c   5979 from 8014

Answer:

_____

d   11 989 from 26 221

Answer:

_____

e   108 767 from 231 111

Answer:

_____

QUESTION 10

Use division to solve the following.

a $2177 \div 7 =$

Answer:

___

b $4484 \div 4 =$

Answer:

___

c $63.9 \div 0.3 =$

Answer:

___

d $121.63 \div 1.2 =$

Answer:

___

e $466.88 \div 0.8$

Answer:

___

The following information is provided for question 11.

To solve using BODMAS, in order from left to right, solve the **B**rackets first, then **O**f, then **D**ivision, then **M**ultiplication, then **A**ddition and lastly **S**ubtraction. The following example has been done for your reference.

EXAMPLE

Solve $(4 \times 7) \times 2 + 6 - 4$.

STEP 1

Solve the Brackets first: $(4 \times 7) = 28$.

STEP 2

No Division so next solve Multiplication: $28 \times 2 = 56$.

STEP 3

Addition is next: $56 + 6 = 62$.

STEP 4

Subtraction is the last process: $62 - 4 = 58$.

FINAL ANSWER:

58

QUESTION 11

Use BODMAS to solve the following.

a $(6 \times 9) \times 5 + 7 - 2 =$

Answer:

___

b $(9 \times 8) \times 4 + 6 - 1 =$

Answer:

___

c $3 \times (5 \times 7) + 11 - 8 =$

Answer:

___

d $6 + 9 - 5 \times (8 \times 3) =$

Answer:

___

e $9 - 7 + 6 \times 3 + (9 \times 6) =$

Answer:

___

f $6 + 9 \times 4 + (6 \times 7) - 21 =$

Answer:

___

Unit 5: Basic Operations

Section A: Addition

QUESTION 1

iStock.com/Avalon_Studio

A concreter checks the lengths of planks to be used for formwork. The planks measure 2 m, 1 m, 3 m and 5 m. What is the total length of the planks?

Answer:

QUESTION 2

Four lengths of steel reinforcement measure 5 m, 8 m, 13 m and 15 m. What is the total length of steel reinforcement?

Answer:

QUESTION 3

Four pallets of 20-kg ready-mix cement bags are delivered to a worksite. Each pallet has a different number of bags on it. The first pallet has eight bags, the second has 14 bags, the third has 16 bags and the fourth has five bags. How many bags of cement have been delivered?

Answer:

QUESTION 4

An agitator truck driver travels 282 km in the first week, 344 km in the second week, 489 km in the third week and 111 km in the fourth week. How many kilometres have been driven over the four weeks?

Answer:

QUESTION 5

Over a month, a concreting company delivers the following number of cubic metres of ready-mix concrete: 32 m^3 in the first week, 47 m^3 in the second week, 57 m^3 in the third week and 59 m^3 in the fourth week. How many cubic metres of concrete have been delivered in total?

Answer:

QUESTION 6

A labourer buys a utility brush for $22, two pairs of safety glasses for $16 and two pairs of gloves for $9. How much has the labourer spent?

Answer:

QUESTION 7

A major construction company orders the following amounts of deformed reinforcing bars for a worksite: 1582 m of N10S, 1099 m of N12S and 617 m of N16S. How many metres have been ordered in total?

Answer:

QUESTION 8

A concreter buys a 14-inch brick saw, which has a 1700W electric motor and a stand and mitre guide, for $1589, three 1.5-m clamped handle screeds for $169 and two 1200-mm levels for $209. How much has been spent?

Answer:

_____

QUESTION 9

The areas of the driveways being constructed for a retirement village are 16 m², 18 m², 8 m² and 11 m². How many square metres of driveway are being cemented?

Answer:

_____

QUESTION 10

A major construction company uses 178 m³ of cement on the first job, 188 m³ on the second job and 93 m³ on the third job. How many cubic metres have been poured?

Answer:

_____

Section B: Subtraction

Short-answer questions

Specific instructions to students

- This section is designed to help you to improve your subtraction skills for basic operations.
- Read the questions below and answer all of them in the spaces provided.
- You may not use a calculator.
- You need to show all working.

QUESTION 1

A concreter has 103 m of N10S deformed reinforcing bar on site. At different stages of the job, the following lengths are used: 52 m, 12 m, 13 m and 11 m. How many metres are left?

Answer:

_____

QUESTION 2

A warehouse has 500 20-kg bags of sand and cement in stock. If 250 bags are delivered to a worksite in one week, and a further 125 bags are delivered the following week, how many bags remain at the warehouse?

Answer:

_____

QUESTION 3

If 243 m³ of cement are poured in one week and 159 m³ are poured in the next week, how many more cubic metres were poured in the first week compared to the second week?

Answer:

_____

QUESTION 4

A commercial block has a total of 90 m² of lawn. Using a square-mouthed shovel, a labourer digs out 27 m² so that concrete can be poured. How many square metres of the lawn remain?

Answer:

_____

9780170474504

QUESTION 5

A top-of-the-range steel wheelbarrow with square corners is advertised for $230. The store manager offers a discount of $27. How much does the customer pay?

Answer:

QUESTION 6

A site manager of a major concreting company orders $5000 of protection gear for the employees. If $2756 is spent on safety boots, long pants and long-sleeved shirts, how much has been spent on the remaining safety gear?

Answer:

QUESTION 7

An area on a building plan totals 96 m². If 44 m² is for the lawn and 17 m² is for gardens, how many square metres is left to be concreted?

Answer:

QUESTION 8

A concreter uses 69 20-kg bags of builders cement over a period of time. If 105 bags were in storage to begin with, how many are left?

Answer:

QUESTION 9

iStock.com/kozmoat98

The odometer of an agitator truck has a reading of 56 089 km at the start of the year. At the end of the year it reads 71 101 km. How many kilometres have been travelled during the year?

Answer:

QUESTION 10

A concreter uses 31 20-kg bags of builders cement on one job, 29 bags on another job and 103 bags on the last job. If there were 250 bags to begin with, how many are left?

Answer:

Section C: Multiplication

Short-answer questions

Specific instructions to students

- This section is designed to help you to improve your multiplication skills for basic operations.
- Read the following questions and answer all of them in the spaces provided.
- You may not use a calculator.
- You need to show all working.

QUESTION 1

A concrete finisher charges $30 per hour. How much is earned for a 45-hour week?

Answer:

QUESTION 2

An apprentice concreter counts 14 20-kg bags of builders cement on a pallet. How many bags would there be on 15 pallets?

Answer:

QUESTION 3

A concreting foreman's van uses 13 litres of diesel for one trip to a worksite. How much fuel is used if the van makes the same trip each day for 18 days?

Answer:

QUESTION 4

A concreter uses 12 m of plank for formwork on a driveway at a housing estate. How many metres of plank are needed for 24 driveways of the same length?

Answer:

QUESTION 5

An apprentice concreter uses 33 bags of ready-mix cement in a week. How many bags does he use over four weeks?

Answer:

QUESTION 6

A concrete finisher uses 16 kg of a 20-kg bag of cement to finish off a path. How many kilograms are needed for 15 of the same finish?

Answer:

QUESTION 7

A labourer's car uses nine litres of LPG every 100 km. How much LPG is used for 450 km?

Answer:

QUESTION 8

If 673 bags of ready-mix cement are used per month by a major concreting company, how many bags are used over a year?

Answer:

QUESTION 9

If a labourer uses eight tubes of inject mortar each day, how many are used during a 31-day month?

Answer:

QUESTION 10

A small concreting business gets a contract in the country and the workers need to travel to the worksite. If they travel at 110 km/h for five hours, how far have they travelled?

Answer:

Section D: Division

Short-answer questions

Specific instructions to students

- This section is designed to help you to improve your division skills for basic operations.
- Read the questions below and answer all of them in the spaces provided.
- You may not use a calculator.
- You need to show all working.

QUESTION 1

A labourer works a total of 24 hours over three days. How many hours are worked each day?

Answer:

QUESTION 2

An experienced concrete-mixing truck driver earns $868 for working a five-day week. How much is earned per day?

Answer:

9780170474504

QUESTION 3

Shutterstock.com/Yoottana Tiyaworanan

To finish off some concrete post work at four different worksites, 140 20-kg bags of cement are needed. How many bags are used at each site if they all need the same amount of cement? Are there any bags left over?

Answer:

_____

QUESTION 4

A concrete-mixing truck covers 780 km in a five-day week. On average, how many kilometres per day have been travelled?

Answer:

_____

QUESTION 5

A company requires 88 20-kg bags of cement to finish some concreting work on four separate worksites. How many bags are allocated evenly to each worksite?

Answer:

_____

QUESTION 6

A concreting foreman gets paid $2926 for seven days of work, including overtime for the weekend. How much does he earn per day?

Answer:

_____

QUESTION 7

A forklift driver at a cement-making company counts 2326 bags of cement. If the bags are stocked in 100 bag lots, how many lots are there? Are there any bags left over?

Answer:

_____

QUESTION 8

A manager orders 408 bags of 20-kg ready-mix cement for a construction company. If the bags are put into six-bag lots at the warehouse, how many lots are there?

Answer:

_____

QUESTION 9

At three separate worksites, a total of $450 \, m^3$ of cement is poured. How many cubic metres are allocated to each of the three sites, if the same amount is poured at each site?

Answer:

_____

QUESTION 10

A concreting foreman travels 2290 km in 28 days, inspecting worksites. On average, how many kilometres are travelled each day?

Answer:

_____

Section A: Addition

QUESTION 1

Some wire mesh measures 6 m long × 2.4 m wide. If there are three grids of wire mesh next to the worksite and they are laid side by side, how wide will they span?

Answer:

QUESTION 2

A concrete contractor purchases an aluminium concrete rake for $39.95, a pair of knee pads for $29.95, a 200-mm steel fixer/concrete nipper tool for $44.55 and a spirit level for $19.45. How much money is spent?

Answer:

QUESTION 3

A 7-inch gauging trowel with a soft grip costs $29.85, a heavy-duty concrete groover tool costs $19.50 and a pair of concreter's nippers costs $15.65. What is the total cost?

Answer:

QUESTION 4

A contractor buys a second-hand 6.5hp concrete trowel machine for $1105.50 and two 3-speed hand-held concrete core drilling machines for $988.50. What is the total cost for all of the items?

Answer:

QUESTION 5

An apprentice buys the following items for work: a grooved plugging chisel for $8.99, a set of steel raker wheels and rivets for $6.50, a #8 50-m lime stringline for $6.50 and a 4.5-inch heavy-duty bolster with wrist guard for $25.99. What is the total cost?

Answer:

QUESTION 6

If a concrete truck driver travels 65.8 km, 36.5 km, 22.7 km and 89.9 km, what is the total distance travelled?

Answer:

QUESTION 7

What is the total length of a driveway that measures 15.5 m and a path that measures 17.8 m?

Answer:

QUESTION 8

At a clearance sale, a 3.6-cu ft heavy-duty petrol mixer with adjustable stand costs $2420.50, and a heavy-duty galvanised electric block saw with a 2.2kW motor and 200-mm depth-of-cut costs $3790.50. What is the total cost for both?

Answer:

QUESTION 9

Three invoices are issued for three completed small concreting jobs. The first invoice is for $450.80, for the first job. The next invoice is for $1130.65, for the second job, and the final invoice is for $660.45, for the last job. What is the total for all three invoices?

Answer:

QUESTION 10

An 18-oz all-steel hammer with a patented rubber Shock-Blok™ head costs $89.90. How much do four cost?

Answer:

Section B: Subtraction

Short-answer questions

Specific instructions to students

- This section is designed to help you to improve your subtraction skills when working with decimals.
- Read the questions below and answer all of them in the spaces provided.
- You may not use a calculator.
- You need to show all working.

QUESTION 1

A forklift driver raises the forklift to a height of 2.5 m. It is then lowered 388 mm, then an extra 295 mm, to move a load. At what height is the forklift, after being lowered for the second time?

Answer:

QUESTION 2

Wire mesh that measures 6 m long × 2.4 m wide has 0.65 m cut off from the width. How wide is it now?

Answer:

QUESTION 3

A concrete finisher completes a job and the company charges $789.20. The boss of the company gives a discount of $75.50 to the client for being a regular customer. How much does the client need to pay?

Answer:

QUESTION 4

A labourer working for a concreting company works 38 hours in a week and earns $729.98. Petrol costs for the week come to $48.85. How much money is left?

Answer:

QUESTION 5

The scaffolding used to reach an outside area of a house being rendered is 3.60 m high. The scaffolding needs to be lowered to a height of 2.95 m to allow work on the next section of the house. How far has the scaffolding been lowered?

Answer:

QUESTION 6

Two lengths need to be cut from a 6-m plank of timber for formwork. The two lengths measure 2.25 m and 2.87 m. How much is left of the 6-m plank of timber?

Answer:

QUESTION 7

A small concreting business has an account balance of $4000.95. The business manager purchases a concreting helicopter (a power trowel machine that finishes screed, has a 42-inch wide kohler and has a 9.5hp motor) for $1950.50. How much is money is left in the company's account?

Answer:

QUESTION 8

A length of timber is used for formwork for a path. The timber measures 1.25 m. If 900 mm is cut from it, how much remains?

Answer:

QUESTION 9

A concreting company has $5000 in the work account. The manager purchases a 1200-mm spirit level for $56.90, a 1.2-m four-stroke concrete finish screed for $369.95 and a 1500W 230v hammer electric power drill for $179.95. How much money is left in the account?

Answer:

QUESTION 10

A concrete finisher gets paid $2280.50 for a fortnight's work. If $350.90 is spent on buying new concreting tools, $44.50 on petrol and $175.50 on food, how much money does the concrete finisher have left?

Answer:

Section C: Multiplication

Short-answer questions

Specific instructions to students

- This section is designed to help you to improve your multiplication skills when working with decimals.
- Read the questions below and answer all of them in the spaces provided.
- You may not use a calculator.
- You need to show all working.

QUESTION 1

If one 20-kg bag of mortar mix costs $7.95, how much do five bags of mortar mix cost?

Answer:

QUESTION 2

An apprentice is asked to purchase 16 bags of 4-kg grey patching mortar that cost $11.25 each, and will be used for finishing work on a house. What is the total cost for all of the bags?

Answer:

QUESTION 3

Two square-mouthed shovels are purchased for $48.96, as well as two square-mouthed post hole shovels for $96.50. What is the total cost?

Answer:

QUESTION 4

A concreter purchases six 8-m fluro green measuring tapes for $8.65 each. What is the total cost?

Answer:

9780170474504

QUESTION 5

A concreter purchases three metal floats with wooden handles, used for finishing render, concreting and screeds, for $29.75 each. What is the total cost?

Answer:

QUESTION 6

A concrete finisher works for a concreting company and earns $30.55 per hour. If 38 hours are worked in one week what is the gross wage (before tax)?

Answer:

QUESTION 7

Large stringline holders have been discounted to $2.55 each. If 25 are purchased, how much money has been spent?

Answer:

QUESTION 8

A construction labourer's car has a 52-litre fuel tank. Unleaded fuel costs $1.35 per litre. How much does it cost the driver to fill the tank if there are only two litres left in it?

Answer:

QUESTION 9

A major concreting company purchases four concrete vibrators (each with a four-stroke 11.5hp petrol engine, a running speed of 7000 rpm, poker length of 1 m, a poker head diameter of 38 mm and weighing 11.5 kg) at a cost of $679.75 each. What is the total cost for all four concrete vibrators?

Answer:

QUESTION 10

Shutterstock.com/Dmitry Kalinovsky

A labourer earns $160.65 per day. What is the gross weekly wage (before tax) for five days of work?

Answer:

Section D: Division

Short-answer questions

Specific instructions to students

- This section is designed to help you to improve your division skills when working with decimals.
- Read the questions below and answer all of them in the spaces provided.
- You may not use a calculator.
- You need to show all working.

QUESTION 1

A cement truck delivers 18.3 m³ of cement to three different worksites in three separate deliveries. How many cubic metres of cement are delivered to each site if they each have the same amount delivered?

Answer:

QUESTION 2

A cement truck makes four trips to a worksite to deliver its load. In total, 23.2 m³ have been delivered. How many cubic metres, on average, are delivered on each trip?

Answer:

QUESTION 3

A concreting company charges $3732.70 to complete the concreting of a driveway and a path near a house. If it has taken 50 hours to complete the job, what is the rate per hour, inclusive of labour and materials?

Answer:

QUESTION 4

A truck driver for a concreting company gets paid $607.23 for 27 hours of driving. What is the hourly rate?

Answer:

QUESTION 5

A cement truck drives from Adelaide to Darwin to replace a truck that has broken down. The driver covers 3368 km in seven days. On average, what distance has been travelled each day?

Answer:

QUESTION 6

A concreting subcontractor scores a job interstate and needs to drive from Adelaide to Melbourne, travelling a total of 889 km to reach the job. The trip takes nine and a half hours of driving time. The driver takes breaks at different stages. What is the average speed for the driving time?

Answer:

QUESTION 7

If 56 20-kg bags of builders cement are required for 3.5 m^3 of finished concrete for a driveway, how many bags are needed per cubic metre?

Answer:

QUESTION 8

If 88 20-kg bags of builders cement are required for 5.5 m^3 of finished concrete for a path, how many bags are needed per cubic metre?

Answer:

QUESTION 9

Shutterstock.com/Kzenon

A forklift driver earns $721.62 for working a 38-hour week. How much is earned per hour?

Answer:

QUESTION 10

If 32.5 20-kg bags of builders cement are required for 2.5 m^3 of finished concrete for foundations, how many bags are required per cubic metre?

Answer:

9780170474504

Unit 7: Fractions

Section A: Addition

Short-answer questions

Specific instructions to students

- This section is designed to help you to improve your addition skills when working with fractions.
- Read the questions below and answer all of them in the spaces provided.
- You may not use a calculator.
- You need to show all working.

QUESTION 1

$\frac{1}{2} + \frac{4}{5} =$

Answer:

QUESTION 2

$2\frac{2}{4} + 1\frac{2}{3} =$

Answer:

QUESTION 3

A labourer puts $\frac{1}{3}$ of a 20-kg cement bag into a mixer. Another $\frac{1}{3}$ of the bag is added. How much of the 20-kg bag has been added to the mixer, as a fraction?

Answer:

QUESTION 4

A concreter puts $\frac{1}{3}$ of a bag of sand into a mixer. Another $\frac{1}{2}$ of the bag is added. How much sand has been used, as a fraction?

Answer:

QUESTION 5

An apprentice adds 1 and $\frac{2}{3}$ bags of cement to a mixer. Another 1 and $\frac{1}{4}$ bags is added. What is the total amount of cement added, as a fraction?

Answer:

iStock.com/majorosl

Section B: Subtraction

Short-answer questions

Specific instructions to students

- This section is designed to help you to improve your subtraction skills when working with fractions.
- Read the questions below and answer all of them in the spaces provided.
- You may not use a calculator.
- You need to show all working.

QUESTION 1

$\frac{2}{3} - \frac{1}{4} =$

Answer:

_____

QUESTION 2

$2\frac{2}{3} - 1\frac{1}{4} =$

Answer:

_____

QUESTION 3

A labourer has $\frac{2}{3}$ of a bag of render. Half a bag is used for a job. How much is left from the original $\frac{2}{3}$ in the bag, as a fraction?

Answer:

_____

QUESTION 4

A cement bag is $\frac{3}{4}$ full. If $\frac{1}{8}$ is used on a job, how much is left, as a fraction?

Answer:

_____

QUESTION 5

There are 2 and $\frac{1}{2}$ bags of sand on site. If 1 and $\frac{1}{3}$ bags are used for a job, how much is left, as a fraction?

Answer:

_____

Section C: Multiplication

Short-answer questions

Specific instructions to students

- This section is designed to help you to improve your multiplication skills when working with fractions.
- Read the questions below and answer all of them in the spaces provided.
- You may not use a calculator.
- You need to show all working.

QUESTION 1

$\frac{2}{4} \times \frac{2}{3} =$

Answer:

_____

QUESTION 2

$2\frac{2}{3} \times 1\frac{1}{2} =$

Answer:

_____

 9780170474504

QUESTION 3

A subcontractor has five half-full 20-kg bags of cement. How many full bags does this make, as a fraction?

Answer:

QUESTION 4

There are 8 and $\frac{1}{2}$ bags of cement on a pallet at a worksite. If each bag weighs 20 kg, how many kilograms are there in total?

Answer:

QUESTION 5

A concrete delivery truck driver works 37 and $\frac{1}{2}$ hours in a week and gets paid $22.50 per hour. How much is earned for the week?

Answer:

Section D: Division

Short-answer questions

Specific instructions to students

- This section is designed to help you to improve your division skills when working with fractions.
- Read the questions below and answer all of them in the spaces provided.
- You may not use a calculator.
- You need to show all working.

QUESTION 1

$\frac{2}{3} \div \frac{1}{4} =$

Answer:

QUESTION 2

$2\frac{3}{4} \div 1\frac{1}{3} =$

Answer:

QUESTION 3

Two batches of wet cement are made up in a wheelbarrow and need to be poured evenly into six post holes. How much of a batch is to be poured into each post hole, using fractions.

Answer:

QUESTION 4

iStock.com/AzmanL

If an apprentice spends 40 hours over a week at a worksite, but only does physical work for $\frac{4}{5}$ of the time, how many hours have been spent doing work?

Answer:

QUESTION 5

A labourer carries 20 kg of mortar mix, over three trips, up a ladder and onto a roof. How many kilograms are carried up the ladder in each trip, as a fraction?

Answer:

Unit 8: Percentages

Short-answer questions

Specific instructions to students

- In this unit, you will be able to practise and improve your skills in working out percentages.
- Read the questions below and answer all of them in the spaces provided.
- You may not use a calculator.
- You need to show all working.

> **10% rule: move the decimal one place to the left to get 10%.**

EXAMPLE

10% of $45.00 is $4.50.

QUESTION 1

Decorative concrete work is completed on a kitchen floor at a cost of $5220.00. The concreting company gives a 10% discount.

a   How much is the discount worth?

Answer:

b   What is the final cost for the job?

Answer:

QUESTION 2

A 500 mm-wide concrete rack costs $135.00. A 10% discount is given during a sale. What is the final cost after 10% is taken off?

Answer:

QUESTION 3

A contractor buys a rotary laser level and detector, complete with staff and tripod, for $698.00. If a 10% discount is given, how much does the level cost?

Answer:

QUESTION 4

A stainless steel rocker groover 1790D concrete tool is on sale for $24.60. A 5% discount is given.

a   How much is the discount worth?

Answer:

b   What is the final price? (Hint: Find 10%, halve it and then subtract it from the overall price.)

Answer:

QUESTION 5

A labourer buys three bullnose stainless steel edgers for a total of $75.75, a 14v cordless drill for $69 and a 13.2-litre pressure concrete sprayer for $335.95.

a   How much is the total?

Answer:

b   How much is paid after a 10% discount?

Answer:

QUESTION 6

iStock.com/Twoellis

A concreter purchases a tie wire twister for $42.55, a 1700w commercial-grade jack hammer for $229.95, a 65 × 600 wood float for $23.99 and a 15m extension lead for $14.99.

a   What is the total?

Answer:

b   What is the final cost after a 10% discount?

Answer:

QUESTION 7

A hardware store offers 20% off the price of 5/8-inch portable handheld manual rebar benders, which normally retail for $402.99. How much will they cost after the discount?

Answer:

QUESTION 8

Cordless drills are discounted by 15%. If the regular retail price is $65.00 each, what is the discounted price?

Answer:

QUESTION 9

The regular retail price of a 125-mm 1400w concrete planer is $506.00. The store has a '20% off' sale. How much will it cost during the sale?

Answer:

QUESTION 10

A 900-mm heavy-duty concrete and mesh bolt cutter costs $245.50. How much does it cost after the store takes off 30% during an end-of-financial-year sale?

Answer:

Unit 9: Measurement Conversions

Short-answer questions

Specific instructions to students

- This unit is designed to help you to improve your skills and to increase your speed in converting one measurement unit into another.
- Read the questions below and answer all of them in the spaces provided.
- You may not use a calculator.
- You need to show all working.

QUESTION 1

How many millimetres are there in 1 cm?

Answer:

QUESTION 2

How many millimetres are there in 1 m?

Answer:

QUESTION 3

How many centimetres are there in 1 m?

Answer:

QUESTION 4

The length of a plank used for formwork is 2550 mm. What is the length in metres?

Answer:

QUESTION 5

The width of a driveway measures 3650 mm. How many metres is this?

Answer:

QUESTION 6

The length of one section of a path is 2.6 m. How many millimetres is this?

Answer:

QUESTION 7

One section of a driveway is 2850 mm in length. Another section is 3250 mm in length. What is the total length of the driveway?

Answer:

QUESTION 8

Three areas of a house need concreting. The areas measure 2.45 m^3, 3.15 m^3 and 1.85 m^3. What is the total area, in cubic metres, to be concreted?

Answer:

QUESTION 9

What is the length of a path to be concreted that has the measurements of 2580 mm along the front section, 3250 mm along the side section and 2400 mm along the back of the house? Answer in millimetres and metres.

Answer:

QUESTION 10

An apprentice concreter is reading from a building plan and considers four areas for concreting. He estimates that the following amounts of concrete are needed: Area 1 is $2.85\,m^3$, Area 2 is $2.35\,m^3$, Area 3 is $2.85\,m^3$ and Area 4 is $23\,m^3$. What are the total cubic metres required according to the estimates?

Answer:

Shutterstock.com/Ramona Heim

Section A: Area

> **Area = length × breadth and is given in square units**
>
> $= l \times b$

QUESTION 1

The dimensions of a driveway are $3\,m \times 12.8\,m$ wide. What is the total area?

Answer:

QUESTION 2

A path measures $2.2\,m \times 11.3\,m$. What is the total area?

Answer:

QUESTION 3

The area for a concrete slab measures $3.5\,m \times 3.65\,m$. What is the total area?

Answer:

QUESTION 4

A toilet floor measures $2.1\,m \times 0.8\,m$. What is the total floor area to be concreted?

Answer:

QUESTION 5

A bedroom measures $3.3\,m \times 3.5\,m$. What is the total area?

Answer:

QUESTION 6

A lounge measures $3.55\,m \times 3.28\,m$. What is the total area of the lounge?

Answer:

QUESTION 7

The measurement of a single carport being concreted is $6.5\,m \times 3.5\,m$. What is the total area of the carport?

Answer:

QUESTION 8

A kitchen measures $5.5\,m \times 4.2\,m$. What is the total area?

Answer:

QUESTION 9

Shutterstock.com/photobank.ch

A garage floor measures 5.2 m wide × 8.6 m long. What is the total floor area?

Answer:

QUESTION 10

A double carport is 9.5 m long × 10.6 m wide. What is the total floor area?

Answer:

Section B: Perimeter

Short-answer questions

Specific instructions to students

- This section is designed to help you to improve your skills and to increase your speed in measuring perimeter.
- Read the questions below and answer all of them in the spaces provided.
- You may not use a calculator.
- You need to show all working.

Perimeter is the length of all sides added together.

> **Perimeter = length + breadth + length + breadth**

The unit of measurement is either in metres, centimetres or millimetres.

QUESTION 1

Calculate the perimeter of a house that is 13 m long × 9 m wide.

Answer:

QUESTION 2

Work out the perimeter of a room that is 3.2 m × 2.6 m.

Answer:

QUESTION 3

What is the perimeter of a lounge that is 4.8 m × 3.8 m?

Answer:

QUESTION 4

Find the perimeter of a carport that is 6.5 m × 2.7 m.

Answer:

QUESTION 5

What is the perimeter of a double carport that measures 6.4 m × 7.7 m?

Answer:

QUESTION 6

Work out the perimeter of a triple carport that is 12.85 m wide × 6.35 m long.

Answer:

QUESTION 7

A pergola to be paved is 4.65 m × 3.85 m. What is the perimeter?

Answer:

iStock.com/JurgaR

QUESTION 8

A dining room has the dimensions of 3.75 m × 3.95 m. What is the perimeter?

Answer:

QUESTION 9

On a building plan, a garage measures 15.55 m × 4.65 m. What is the perimeter?

Answer:

QUESTION 10

A path around a rectangular pool has two sides that are 11.75 m and two sides that are 6.95 m. What is the total perimeter?

Answer:

Section C: Volume – paths, driveways and garage floors

Short-answer questions

Specific instructions to students

- This section is designed to help you to improve your skills and to increase your speed in measuring the volume of paths, driveways and garage floors.
- Read the questions below and answer all of them in the spaces provided.
- You may not use a calculator.
- You need to show all working.

> **Volume = length × width × thickness ÷ 1000, and is given in cubic metres**

Use the following minimum thickness values to solve the following questions.

- Paths – 75 mm
- Driveways – 100 mm
- Garage floors – 125 mm.

QUESTION 1

If the floor dimensions of an equipment storage shed are 13 m × 5 m × 4 m, how many cubic metres are there?

Answer:

QUESTION 2

Alamy Stock Photo/David R. Frazier Photolibrary, Inc.

On a building plan, a driveway has the dimensions of 15 m × 3 m. How many cubic metres of concrete are needed?

Answer:

QUESTION 3

A garage floor measures 9 m long × 8 m wide. How many cubic metres is the floor?

Answer:

QUESTION 4

Two new paths are being concreted at a shopping mall. Each path measures 22.2 m long × 1.8 m wide. How many cubic metres of concrete are needed?

Answer:

QUESTION 5

A new house needs a driveway built to accommodate several cars. The driveway measures 15 m × 7 m. How many cubic metres of concrete are needed?

Answer:

QUESTION 6

A new double garage floor is 8 m × 8 m. How many cubic metres of concrete are needed?

Answer:

QUESTION 7

A path around a rectangular garden feature is being concreted. The feature has sides that are 5.5 m × 4.8 m. The width of the path is 1 m and the thickness is 75 mm. What is the amount of concrete required to complete the path, in cubic metres?

Answer:

QUESTION 8

A major shopping mall needs eight new paths constructed. Each path measures 18.5 m × 1.8 m. How many cubic metres of concrete are needed for all eight paths?

Answer:

QUESTION 9

The driveway of a house in a new estate has two separate lengths of concrete slab. Each slab measures 7.5 m × 1.3 m. How many cubic metres of concrete are needed for both slabs?

Answer:

QUESTION 10

A client wants to pour concrete for a new driveway, garage floor and path. The dimensions of each are 8.5 m × 3.4 m, 7.8 m × 3.4 m and 1.2 m × 3.4 m. Calculate the total cubic metres of concrete needed.

Answer:

Unit 10: Measurement – Area, Perimeter and Volume **29**

Section D: Volume – circles and triangles

> **Area of a circle = Pi (use π = 3.14) × radius squared × thickness ÷ 1000**
>
> **Area of a triangle = $\frac{1}{2}$ × base × height × thickness ÷ 1000**

QUESTION 1

Shutterstock.com/Ru Bai Le

A circular area with a radius of 1 m and a thickness of 75 mm is being concreted. How many cubic metres of concrete are needed?

Answer:

QUESTION 2

A circular area with a radius of 2 m and a thickness of 100 mm is being concreted. How many cubic metres of concrete are needed?

Answer:

QUESTION 3

A circular area with a diameter of 3 m and a thickness of 125 mm is being concreted. How many cubic metres of concrete are needed?

Answer:

QUESTION 4

A circular area with a radius of 5 m and a thickness of 75 mm is being concreted. How many cubic metres of concrete are needed?

Answer:

QUESTION 5

A triangular area with a base of 1 m, a width of 2 m and a thickness of 75 mm is being concreted. How many cubic metres of concrete are needed?

Answer:

QUESTION 6

A triangular area with a base of 2 m, a width of 2 m and a thickness of 100 mm is being concreted. How many cubic metres of concrete are needed?

Answer:

QUESTION 7

A triangular area with a base of 3 m, a width of 3 m and a thickness of 125 mm is being concreted. How many cubic metres of concrete are needed?

Answer:

QUESTION 8

Two circular areas, one with a radius of 1.5 m and the other with a radius of 2 m, and both with a thickness of 75 mm, are being concreted. How many cubic metres of concrete are needed for both areas?

Answer:

QUESTION 9

Three floor areas of an outside public space are planned to be concrete areas. The first is a rectangle area that measures 13 m × 4.5 m, the second area is square-shaped and measures 6.5 m × 6.5 m, and the third area is triangular-shaped and has a base of 5.5 m and a width of 5.5 m. The thickness for all areas is 100 mm. How many cubic metres of concrete are needed for all three areas?

Answer:

QUESTION 10

Five new areas of a shopping mall floor have been designed as the following shapes: a rectangle that is 16.5 m × 6.5 m, two circles with the radiuses measuring 2.5 m, and two triangles with the bases measuring 5.5 m and the width measuring 4.5 m. The thickness for all areas is 100 mm. How many cubic metres of concrete are needed for all five areas?

Answer:

Section E: Volume – post holes

Short-answer questions

Specific instructions to students

- This section is designed to help you to improve your skills and to increase your speed in measuring the volume of post holes.
- Read the questions below and answer all of them in the spaces provided.
- You may not use a calculator.
- You need to show all working.

Use the following equations to calculate the volume of concrete needed for holes for round galvanised posts and rectangular timber posts.

Round galvanised hollow posts into a cylindrical hole

Volume of the hole = Pi (use π = 3.14) × radius squared × depth

Rectangular timber posts into a rectangular hole

Volume of a rectangular post = width × breadth × length (in hole)

Volume of a rectangular hole = 2w × 2b × depth

Volume of hole – volume of the post = cement needed

QUESTION 1

A round galvanised hollow steel fence post needs to be replaced. The post measures 37 mm in diameter and is 2400 mm long. The hole needs to be twice as wide as the diameter of the pole and 600 mm deep. Calculate the volume of concrete needed for the hole, in cubic metres.

Answer:

QUESTION 2

Cengage Learning Australia/Sian Bradfield

A round galvanised hollow steel fence post needs to be replaced. The post measures 50 mm in diameter and is 1.8 m in height. The hole needs to be twice as wide as the diameter of the pole and 800 mm deep. Calculate the volume of concrete needed for the hole, in cubic metres.

Answer:

_____

_____

_____

QUESTION 3

Twenty round galvanised hollow steel fence posts need to be cemented for a fence. Each post measures 37 mm in diameter and is 2800 mm in height. Each hole needs to be twice as wide as the diameter of the pole and 800 mm deep.

a Calculate the volume of concrete needed for each hole, in cubic metres.

Answer:

_____

_____

_____

b Calculate the total volume of concrete needed for all 20 posts?

Answer:

_____

_____

QUESTION 4

A rectangular timber post needs to be replaced. The post measures 75 mm × 75 mm × 2.4 m. One-third of the post will be cemented into the hole.

a What is the volume of the post?

Answer:

_____

_____

b The hole needs to be twice the breadth and width of the post, and with a depth of 800 mm. What is the volume of the hole?

Answer:

_____

_____

c Subtract the volume of the post from the volume of the hole to calculate how much cement is needed for the job. Give your answer in cubic metres.

Answer:

_____

_____

QUESTION 5

A rectangular treated-timber post needs to be replaced. The post measures 90 mm × 90 mm × 2.4 m. One-third of the post will be cemented into the hole.

a What is the volume of the post?

Answer:

_____

_____

b The hole needs to be twice the breadth and width of the post, and with a depth of 800 mm. What is the volume of the hole?

Answer:

_____

_____

c What is the volume of the concrete needed to set the post? Give your answer in cubic metres.

Answer:

_____

_____

QUESTION 6

A rectangular timber post needs to be replaced. The post measures 100 mm × 100 mm × 2.4 m. One-third of the post will be cemented into the hole.

a What is the volume of the post?

Answer:

_____

_____

b The hole needs to be twice the breadth and width of the post. The depth of the whole will be 800 mm. What is the volume of the hole?

Answer:

_____

_____

c What is the volume of cement needed to set the post? Give your answer in cubic metres.

Answer:

_____

_____

QUESTION 7

Twenty rectangular treated-timber posts need to be put in to build a new fence. The posts measure 75 mm × 75 mm × 2.4 m. Each hole needs to be twice the breadth and width of the post, and the depth of the hole will be 800 mm. What is the volume of concrete needed to set the 20 posts?

Answer:

_____

_____

_____

_____

_____

_____

QUESTION 8

Draw a diagram to assist with solving the following question. (Use the 'Notes' pages at the back of this book.)

A boundary fence at a school is being constructed. The principal wants the fence to be 16 m long, the posts to be 1800 mm high, 100 mm in diameter, and 2 m apart, erected and cemented into 600-mm deep cylindrical holes in the ground using round galvanised hollow posts.

a How many posts are needed?

Answer:

_____

b Calculate the amount of cement needed for each hole.

Answer:

_____

_____

_____

_____

c How much cement is needed in total?

Answer:

_____

QUESTION 9

Getty Images/Dorling Kindersley

A fence on a farm needs 12 rectangular treated-timber posts to be erected. Each post measures 90 mm × 90 mm × 2.4 m.

a If a third of the post is being cemented in the hole, what is the required depth, in metres?

Answer:

_____

b The breadth and width of the hole needs to be twice the breadth and width of the post. Calculate the volume of the hole. (Allow 100 mm depth for gravel under the timber post for drainage.)

Answer:

_____

_____

_____

_____

c How many cubic metres of cement are needed for each hole?

Answer:

_____

_____

d How much cement is needed for all 12 posts?

Answer:

_____

QUESTION 10

A fence with 125 rectangular treated-pine posts is being erected using 100 mm × 100 mm × 2.4 m posts.

a If a third of the post is being cemented in the hole, what is the required depth, in metres?

Answer:

_____

b The breadth and width of the hole needs to be twice the breadth and width of the post. Calculate the volume of the hole. (Allow 100 mm depth for gravel under the timber post for drainage.)

Answer:

_____

_____

_____

_____

c How many cubic metres of cement are needed for each hole?

Answer:

_____

_____

d How much cement is needed for all 125 posts?

Answer:

_____

9780170474504

Unit 11: Earning Wages

Short-answer questions

Specific instructions to students

- This unit is designed to help you to calculate how much a job is worth and how long you need to complete the job.
- Read the questions below and answer all of them in the spaces provided.
- You may not use a calculator.
- You need to show all working.

Hourly wages

Concrete finisher – $30.00

Labourer – $19.21

Concrete-mixing truck driver – $22.49

Concreting foreman – $34.00

Construction labourer – $20.00

Forklift driver – $18.99

Concrete-pump operator – $29.75

Use the above information to calculate the answers to the following questions.

QUESTION 1

A concrete finisher works seven and a half hours per day for five days. How much is earned for the week, before tax?

Answer:

QUESTION 2

A labourer works seven and a half hours per day for five days. How much is earned for the week, before tax?

Answer:

QUESTION 3

A concrete-mixing truck driver works seven and a half hours per day for five days. How much is earned for the week, before tax?

Answer:

QUESTION 4

A concreting foreman works seven and a half hours per day for 10 days. How much is earned for the fortnight, before tax?

Answer:

QUESTION 5

A construction labourer gets paid monthly and works a total of 152 hours for the month. How much is earned for the month, before tax?

Answer:

QUESTION 6

A forklift driver gets paid monthly and works 150 hours every month.

a   How much is the gross wage for the month?

Answer:

b   What is the gross yearly wage?

Answer:

QUESTION 7

Three concrete-mixing truck drivers each work a total of 75 hours over a fortnight. How much does their employer need to pay, in total, for the three wages, before tax?

Answer:

QUESTION 8

A forklift driver works 150 hours over a month, as per the normal hours required by the company employing her. An extra 10 hours are also worked at time-and-a-half. How much is earned for the month, before tax?

Answer:

_____

QUESTION 9

A concreting foreman gets paid monthly and works 150 hours every month.

a How much is the gross wage for the month?

Answer:

_____

b What is the gross yearly wage?

Answer:

_____

QUESTION 10

iStock.com/Avalon_Studio

A concrete-pump operator works 37.5 hours over a week. The operator works overtime for eight hours on Saturday at a rate of $44.63. How much is the gross earnings for the working week, including overtime?

Answer:

_____

Unit 12: Squaring Numbers

Section A: Introducing square numbers

Short-answer questions

Specific instructions to students

- This section is designed to help you to improve your skills and to increase your speed in squaring numbers.
- Read the questions below and answer all of them in the spaces provided.
- You may not use a calculator.
- You need to show all working.

Any number squared is multiplied by itself.

EXAMPLE

4 squared $= 4^2 = 4 \times 4 = 16$

QUESTION 1

$6^2 =$

Answer:

QUESTION 2

$8^2 =$

Answer:

QUESTION 3

$12^2 =$

Answer:

QUESTION 4

$3^2 =$

Answer:

QUESTION 5

$7^2 =$

Answer:

QUESTION 6

$11^2 =$

Answer:

QUESTION 7

$10^2 =$

Answer:

QUESTION 8

$9^2 =$

Answer:

QUESTION 9

$2^2 =$

Answer:

QUESTION 10

$14^2 =$

Answer:

Section B: Applying square numbers to the trade

Worded practical problems

Specific instructions to students

- This section is designed to help you to improve your skills and to increase your speed in calculating the volume of rectangular or square objects. The worded questions make the content relevant to everyday situations.
- Read the questions below and answer all of them in the spaces provided.
- You may not use a calculator.
- You need to show all working.

QUESTION 1

The floor of a pergola area measures 2.8 m × 2.8 m. What is the total area, in square metres?

Answer:

QUESTION 2

An outdoor area that will be concreted with decorative cement is 5.2 m × 5.2 m. What is the total area, in square metres?

Answer:

QUESTION 3

The dimensions of a bedroom floor being renovated, jackhammered and concreted are 3.6 m × 3.6 m. What is the total floor area to be cemented, in square metres?

Answer:

QUESTION 4

A slab needs to be poured for a storage area for concrete-work machinery and equipment. The floor area measures 15 m × 15 m. A smaller slab for a shed also needs to be poured and the area measures 3.4 m × 3.4 m. What is the total floor area, in square metres?

Answer:

QUESTION 5

A house being built has a total floor area of 13.8 m × 13.8 m. How much square area is the house?

Answer:

QUESTION 6

Alamy Stock Photo/imageBROKER/Daniel Schoenen

A shower recess measures 2.4 m × 2.4 m and is jackhammered during a renovation. Screed is laid in the recess. The conjoining bedroom floor measures 3.8 m × 3.8 m and is joined to the bathroom. How many square metres in total are the two areas?

Answer:

QUESTION 7

During a renovation, a patio area and outdoor entertainment area are jackhammered, demolished and replaced with decorative concrete. If the patio area is 3.8 m × 3.8 m and the outdoor entertainment area is 6.8 m × 6.8 m, how many square metres are being concreted?

Answer:

9780170474504

QUESTION 8

A garage floor and a shed floor have been jackhammered and demolished and are being replaced with concrete. The garage floor measures 8.5 m × 8.5 m. The shed floor is 4.25 m × 4.25 m. How many square metres in total are the two floors?

Answer:

QUESTION 9

Three areas at a factory are being demolished and replaced with concrete. Each area has different dimensions. The first area is an expansive storage area and measures 45 m × 45 m. The second area is a docking bay for loading goods and measures 13 m × 13 m. The third area is an office area that measures 3.5 m × 3.5 m. How many square metres in total for all three areas?

Answer:

QUESTION 10

A warehouse is being built for a major hardware store and the floor area measures 59.5 m × 59.5 m. What is the total area, in square metres?

Answer:

Shutterstock.com/Ari N

Unit 13: Ratios

Short-answer questions

Specific instructions to students

- This unit is designed to help you to improve your skills and to increase your speed in calculating and simplifying ratios.
- Read the questions below and answer all of them in the spaces provided.
- You may not use a calculator.
- You need to show all working.
- Reduce the ratios to the simplest or lowest form.

QUESTION 1

To make a batching mix of high-strength concrete with improved water tightness, a concreter uses the ratio of 1 part cement, 1.5 parts sand and 3 parts aggregate. If 5 kg of cement needs to be mixed, how many kilograms of sand and aggregate are needed?

Answer:

QUESTION 2

Using the ratio to make high-strength concrete from question 1, how much sand and aggregate are needed if 10 kg of cement is in the batching mix?

Answer:

QUESTION 3

Using the ratio to make high-strength concrete from question 1, how much sand and aggregate are needed if 15 kg of cement is in the batching mix?

Answer:

QUESTION 4

To make a batching mix of concrete for paths, driveways, patios and floors, a concreter uses the ratio of 1 part cement, 2 parts sand and 3 parts aggregate. If 7 kg of cement needs to be mixed, how many kilograms of sand and aggregate are needed?

Answer:

QUESTION 5

Using the ratio to make concrete from question 4, how much sand and aggregate are needed if 12 kg of cement is in the batching mix?

Answer:

QUESTION 6

Using the ratio to make concrete from question 4, how much sand and aggregate are needed if 20 kg of cement is in the batching mix?

Answer:

QUESTION 7

To make a batching mix of concrete for foundations and footings, a concreter uses the ratio of 1 part cement, 3 parts sand and 3 parts aggregate. If 15 kg of cement needs to be mixed, how many kilograms of sand and aggregate are needed?

Answer:

QUESTION 8

Using the ratio to make concrete from question 7, how much sand and aggregate are needed if 50 kg of cement is in the batching mix?

Answer:

QUESTION 9

To make a batching mix of concrete for finishing work on a driveway, a concreter uses the ratio of 1 part cement, 2 parts sand and 3 parts aggregate. If 12 kg of concrete needs to be mixed, how many kilograms of each part are needed?

Answer:

_____

QUESTION 10

Using the ratio to make concrete from question 9, how many kilograms of each part are needed if 36 kg of concrete needs to be mixed?

Answer:

_____

Shutterstock.com/VanderWolfImages

Section A: The apprentice years

QUESTION 1

A first-year apprentice concreter gets paid $12.19 per hour. A travel allowance of $13.07 is also paid per day. If the apprentice works for 31 hours over four days, how much is earned for the working week, including allowances, before tax?

Answer:

QUESTION 2

Shutterstock.com/Monkey Business Images

A first-year apprentice concreter gets paid $12.19 per hour. A travel allowance of $13.07 is also paid per day. If the apprentice works for 62 hours over an eight-day fortnight, how much is earned for the fortnight, including allowances, before tax?

Answer:

QUESTION 3

A first-year apprentice concreter gets paid $12.19 per hour. A travel allowance of $13.07 is also paid per day. If the apprentice works for 124 hours over a 16-day month, how much is earned for the month, including allowances, before tax?

Answer:

QUESTION 4

A first-year apprentice concreter gets paid $12.19 per hour. A travel allowance of $13.07 is also paid per day. The apprentice works for 31 hours over a four-day week. If $50 is spent on petrol, $38 on food and $57 on entertainment, how much money is left over?

Answer:

QUESTION 5

A first-year apprentice concreter gets paid $12.19 per hour, with an additional travel allowance of $13.01 per day. The apprentice works for 31 hours over a four-day week. If $35.50 is spent on petrol, $47.50 on food and $62.75 on entertainment, how much money is left over?

Answer:

QUESTION 6

A second-year apprentice concreter gets paid $14.18 per hour, plus $14.82 per day for a travel allowance. The apprentice works for 31 hours over a four-day week. How much is earned, including allowances, before tax?

Answer:

QUESTION 7

A second-year apprentice concreter gets paid $14.18 per hour, plus $14.82 per day for a travel allowance. The apprentice works for a 62 hours over an eight-day fortnight. How much is earned, including allowances, before tax?

Answer:

9780170474504

QUESTION 8

A second-year apprentice concreter gets paid $14.18 per hour, plus $14.82 per day for a travel allowance. The apprentice works for 124 hours over a 16-day month. How much is earned, including allowances, before tax?

Answer:

QUESTION 9

A second-year apprentice concreter gets paid $14.18 per hour, plus $14.82 per day for a travel allowance. The apprentice works for 31 hours over four days. If $86 is spent on tools, $49 on PPE gear and $18 on medical insurance, how much money is left?

Answer:

QUESTION 10

A second-year apprentice concreter gets paid $14.18 per hour, plus $14.82 per day for a travel allowance. The apprentice works for 62 hours over an eight-day fortnight. The apprentice's fortnightly expenses include: $45.50 for clothes, $42.90 for food and $180.50 for car registration. How much money is left after all the expenses?

Answer:

Section B: Time and motion

Short-answer questions

Specific instructions to students

- This section is designed to help you to improve your Maths skills in the concreting trade.
- Read the questions below and answer all of them in the spaces provided.
- You may not use a calculator.
- You need to show all working.

QUESTION 1

A concrete-mixing truck driver delivers some of the 6 m³ of concrete from his truck to four different sites during the day. The truck arrives at the first site at 7 a.m. to pour the concrete. The first pour takes 53 minutes, the second pour takes 33 minutes, the third pour takes 42 minutes and the last pour takes 29 minutes. How long does it take the truck driver to complete all four concrete pours? Give your answer in hours and minutes.

Answer:

iStock.com/Roel Smart

QUESTION 2

A concrete finisher starts work at 7 a.m. and stops for a break at 9.30 a.m. for 20 minutes. Lunch starts at 11.15 a.m. and is for 30 minutes. The concrete finisher then works until 2 p.m. How many hours have been worked, including breaks?

Answer:

QUESTION 3

A casual concreter earns $35.00 an hour and works a 38-hour week. How much is the weekly gross earnings, before tax?

Answer:

QUESTION 4

Over a week, an apprentice working for a small concreting company completes five jobs. After completing the work, she issues invoices for $465.80, $2490.50, $556.20, $1560.70 and $990.60. What is the total to be paid for all of the completed jobs?

Answer:

QUESTION 5

A labourer takes 34 minutes to unload materials and tools from the work van. It takes eight minutes to plug in the electrical tools and 39 minutes to spread and finish one batch of concrete in a small area. How much time has been taken on this job? Give your answer in hours and minutes.

Answer:

QUESTION 6

A house is being demolished and the driveway and path are being removed. It takes four and a half hours for the two labourers to jackhammer and remove the concrete from the driveway and path. If the company charges a rate of $28.60 an hour for each labourer, what is the bill for this work?

Answer:

QUESTION 7

An apprentice is employed to build a fence. She uses a post-hole digger to dig holes for 75 mm × 75 mm timber posts. She also completes the setting in and cementing of the posts. She works for a total of 7.5 hours. If her pay rate is $14.80 per hour, what is the total bill for her work?

Answer:

QUESTION 8

A concreter digs out an area of lawn that measures 3.5 m × 3.5 m, which takes him 95 minutes. He then constructs formwork around the perimeter, which takes him 35 minutes. It takes him 13 minutes to rake the base, and 14 minutes to pour to base course and rake it. He uses a compactor over the area for 19 minutes, and then for 13 minutes, he spreads a layer of sand and rakes it. It takes him 11 minutes to spread a sheet of polythene over the top and place wire mesh over the sheet. He then pours concrete and spreads it, which takes 43 minutes. He taps the formwork to remove any air, then he screeds the concrete, which takes 44 minutes. He uses a steel trowel to finish off the work, which takes 55 minutes, and he leaves the slab to cure.

How long does it take to complete the job? Give your answer in hours and minutes?

Answer:

QUESTION 9

A work crew begins work at 7.00 a.m. and works until 2.30 p.m. The crew take a morning break for 20 minutes, a lunch break for 30 minutes and an afternoon break for 20 minutes.

a How much time has been spent on breaks?

Answer:

b How much time has been spent working?

Answer:

QUESTION 10

The cost of labour on a concreting job is $960.00. The concreter spends 24 hours on the job. How much is the rate of pay per hour?

Answer:

Section C: Interpreting tables

Thickness (mm)

	50	75	100	125	150
5	0.4	0.4	0.6	0.8	0.8
10	0.6	0.8	1	1.4	1.6
15	0.8	1.2	1.6	2	2.4
20	1	1.6	2	2.6	3
25	1.4	2	2.6	3.2	3.8
30	1.6	2.4	3	3.8	4.6
35	1.8	2.6	3.6	4.4	5.4
40	2	3	4	5	6
45	2.4	3.4	4.6	5.8	6.8
50	2.6	3.8	5	6.4	7.6

Area (m²)

Use the above information to answer the following questions.

QUESTION 1

How many cubic metres of concrete are needed for an area of 5 m² and 75 mm thick?

Answer:

QUESTION 2

How many cubic metres of concrete are needed for an area of 30 m² and 125 mm thick?

Answer:

QUESTION 3

How many cubic metres of concrete are needed for an area of 45 m² and 100 mm thick?

Answer:

QUESTION 4

How many cubic metres of concrete are needed for an area of 15 m² and 150 mm thick?

Answer:

QUESTION 5

How many cubic metres of concrete are needed for an area of 50 m² and 75 mm thick?

Answer:

QUESTION 6

What is the maximum amount of square metres that can be concreted within 4 m³, to a depth of 100 mm?

Answer:

QUESTION 7

What is the maximum amount of square metres that can be concreted within 3 m³, to a depth of 150 mm?

Answer:

_____

QUESTION 8

What is the maximum amount of square metres that can be concreted within 1.4 m³, to a depth of 50 mm?

Answer:

_____

QUESTION 9

What is the maximum amount of square metres that can be concreted within 2.6 m³, to a depth of 50 mm?

Answer:

_____

QUESTION 10

What is the maximum amount of square metres that can be concreted within 7.6 m³, to a depth of 150 mm?

Answer:

_____

Shutterstock.com/Joseph Sohm

9780170474504

Concreting
Practice Written Exam for the Concreting Trade

Reading time: 10 minutes

Writing time: 1 hour 30 minutes

Section A: Literacy

Section B: General Mathematics

Section C: Trade Mathematics

QUESTION and ANSWER BOOK

Section	Topic	Number of questions	Marks
A	Literacy	7	22
B	General Mathematics	11	26
C	Trade Mathematics	44	52
		Total 62	**Total 100**

The sections may be completed in the order of your choice.

NO CALCULATORS are to be used during the exam.

Spelling

Read the passage below and then underline the 10 spelling errors.

10 marks

Formwork acts as a mould for fresh concrete. The most comonly used product for formwork is 25 mm-thick timber, which can be cut to size depending on the foundation needed. The timber needs to be clean and strong enough to suport the waight of the concrete without bending. A builder's square is used to check that the cornars are at right angles and are sturdy. The inside of the timber used for formwork should be oiled before the concrete is laid. If this is not done, the formwork is difficult to remove once the concrete has set. If a drainidge slope is required, the formwork needs to be hamered into the ground to create a slight gradiant. Use timber screads to level out the concrete. Ensure that these are clean for a neat finish.

If the concrete is going to be subjected to heavy foot trafic, it needs to be reinforced with steel or mesh. The concreter needs to consider how much steel is required and where it will be placed to give the concrete the most support. As a genaral rule, two-thirds of the concrete should be below the reinforcing steel and one-third of the concrete on top. Reinforcing steel needs to be placed at least 50 mm below the surface of the concrete.

Correct the spelling errors by writing them out with the correct spelling below.

_____

_____

Alphabetising

Put the following words into alphabetical order.

7 marks

Pour	Slab
Reinforcement	Lime
Aggregate	Safety boots
Waterproofing	Gloves
Wire mesh	Formwork
Concrete	Sand
Trowel	Cement mixer

_____

_____

_____

_____

_____

_____

_____

_____

_____

_____

_____

_____

_____

Comprehension

Short-answer questions

Specific instructions to students

- Read the following passage and answer the questions using full sentences.

Concrete can be mixed with a concrete mixer or by hand, with the use of a bucket or wheelbarrow and a shovel. For bigger jobs a concrete mixer may be required. Mixers can be hired from most hire companies.

Concrete and mortar quantities depend on the features of a project and on its planned sizes and shapes. One common mistake people make is to add too much water to the concrete, which weakens the final product. It is important to use a shovel or screed board to compact the concrete once it has been laid. This helps to remove any bubbles within the concrete. A float or trowel is used to smooth the surface, which needs to be done as quickly as possible. The mix is the most important factor for making strong concrete that is workable. Water only needs to be added as required and too much water will detract from the strength of the concrete. Add a little water at a time to make the consistency of the concrete close to the correct strength.

Some clients like to have coloured concrete. This is done in two ways. Either pigments are added to the mix or the concrete surface is painted. Generally, the best pigments to be added are metallic oxides, which give a truer colour overall. As a rule, a concreter should ensure that the amount of oxide mixed in is no greater than 10 per cent of the cement weight. Sand and gravel can be added once the mixture is consistent and the colour is evenly distributed throughout the mix.
An array of colours can be achieved with the use of a grey cement, off-white cement or white cement.

QUESTION 1   1 mark

What tools are needed when mixing concrete without a mixer?

Answer:

_____

_____

QUESTION 2   1 mark

What is a common mistake people make when mixing concrete?

Answer:

_____

_____

QUESTION 3   1 mark

What tools are used to remove bubbles from concrete once it has been laid?

Answer:

_____

_____

QUESTION 4   1 mark

What are the two ways of colouring concrete?

Answer:

_____

_____

QUESTION 5   1 mark

How much metallic oxide should be added to the weight of the concrete to colour it?

Answer:

_____

_____

Section B: General Mathematics

QUESTION 1   1 + 1 + 1 = 3 marks

What unit of measurement is used to measure:

a   the perimeter of an area for formwork?

Answer:

_____

b   the compression strength of concrete?

Answer:

_____

c   the amount of concrete needed for a driveway?

Answer:

_____

QUESTION 2   1 + 1 + 1 = 3 marks

Give examples of how the following might be used in the concreting trade.

a   Percentage

Answer:

_____

b   Decimals

Answer:

_____

b   Fractions

Answer:

_____

QUESTION 3   1 + 1 = 2 marks

Convert the following units.

a   1 kg to grams

Answer:

_____

b   1500 g to kilograms

Answer:

_____

QUESTION 4   2 marks

Write the following in descending order.

0.7   0.71   7.1   70.1   701.00   7.0

Answer:

_____

QUESTION 5   1 + 1 = 2 marks

Write the decimal number that is between:

a   0.1 and 0.2

Answer:

_____

b   1.3 and 1.4

Answer:

_____

QUESTION 6   1 + 1 = 2 marks

Round off the following numbers to two (2) decimal places.

a   5.177

Answer:

_____

b   12.655

Answer:

_____

QUESTION 7   1 + 1 = 2 marks

Estimate the following by approximation.

a 101×81

Answer:

_____

b 399×21

Answer:

_____

QUESTION 8   1 + 1 = 2 marks

What do the following add up to?

a $25, $13.50 and $165.50

Answer:

_____

b $4, $5.99 and $229.50

Answer:

_____

QUESTION 9   1 + 1 = 2 marks

Subtract the following.

a   196 from 813

Answer:

_____

b   5556 from 9223

Answer:

_____

QUESTION 10   1 + 1 = 2 marks

Use division to solve the following.

a $4824 \div 3 =$

Answer:

_____

b $84.2 \div 0.4 =$

Answer:

_____

QUESTION 11   2 + 2 = 4 marks

Using BODMAS, solve the following.

a $(3 \times 7) \times 4 + 9 - 5 =$

Answer:

_____

b $(8 \times 12) \times 2 + 8 - 4 =$

Answer:

_____

Section C: Trade Mathematics

Basic Operations

Addition

QUESTION 1   1 mark

A concreter purchases 36 20-kg bags of high-strength concrete, 144 3.2 mm × 40 mm concrete nails and 15 4-L buckets of concrete floor sealer. How many items have been purchased in total?

Answer:

QUESTION 2   1 mark

A concreter purchases the following three specialist concreting tools: clear multi-purpose builder's film for $25, concrete spreader with pole for $45 and a spirit level for $17. What is the total cost?

Answer:

Subtraction

QUESTION 1   1 mark

A concreter cuts off 900 mm from a plank that measures 2400 mm, to use for formwork. How many millimetres remain of the plank?

Answer:

QUESTION 2   1 mark

An apprentice purchases PPE gear and the total comes to $124. The manager of the shop takes off a discount of $35 during a sale. How much does the apprentice pay?

Answer:

Multiplication

QUESTION 1   1 mark

A forklift driver shifts five pallets of 15-kg multi-purpose floor leveller. Each pallet has 36 bags on it. How many bags are on the five pallets, in total?

Answer:

QUESTION 2   1 mark

A concreting company uses 250 20-kg bags of concrete mix in the first month, 200 bags in the second month and 160 bags in the third month. How many 20-kg bags have been used, in total?

Answer:

Division

QUESTION 1   1 mark

An invoice for a completed concreting job comes to $5578, which is the cost of labour and materials used to complete demolition and renovations on a short driveway. If the work took six days to complete, what is the average cost per day?

Answer:

QUESTION 2   1 mark

At a yearly stocktake, a store-person counts 72 20-kg bags of high-strength concrete. If 12 bags are packed onto each pallet, how many pallets are there?

Answer:

Decimals

Addition

QUESTION 1   1 mark

A labourer purchases a concrete nipper/steel fixer for $39.95, a 900-mm bull float for $62.50 and a concrete vibrator finisher for $154.50. How much is charged for the purchase?

Answer:

_____

QUESTION 2   1 mark

An online store sells aluminium concrete screed for $79.95, a 240v 1050W cement mixer for $111.50 and a 900-mm finishing trowel for $112.85. What is the total cost for the items?

Answer:

_____

Subtraction

QUESTION 1   1 mark

A casual labourer earns $418.50 for two days of work. She spends $35.95 on clothes and $25.50 on food? How much money is left?

Answer:

_____

QUESTION 2   1 mark

A supervisor of a concreting company purchases a blue steel wheelbarrow for $124.50. If it is paid for with three $50 notes, how much change is given?

Answer:

_____

Multiplication

QUESTION 1   2 marks

A contractor buys three spinner floats for $37.95 each at a sale.

a   How much does it cost for the three floats?

Answer:

_____

b   How much change is given from $150.00?

Answer:

_____

QUESTION 2   2 marks

Four post-hole shovels, with long fiberglass handles, are purchased at a cost of $28.50 each.

a   How much does it cost for the shovels?

Answer:

_____

b   How much change is given from $120.00?

Answer:

_____

Division

QUESTION 1   1 mark

The concrete finisher earns $987.00 for five days of work. How much is earned per day?

Answer:

_____

QUESTION 2   1 mark

Four 355 mm × 100 mm pointed floor trowels cost $88.80. What is the cost of each?

Answer:

_____

Fractions

QUESTION 1   1 mark

$\frac{1}{4} + \frac{1}{2} =$

Answer:

_____

QUESTION 2   1 mark

$\frac{4}{5} - \frac{1}{3} =$

Answer:

_____

QUESTION 3   1 mark

$\frac{2}{3} \times \frac{1}{4} =$

Answer:

_____

QUESTION 4   1 mark

$\frac{3}{4} \div \frac{1}{2} =$

Answer:

_____

Percentages

QUESTION 1   1 mark

A tool company has a '10% off' sale on all items. If a customer's purchase totals $149.00, what is the final sale price once 10% has been taken off?

Answer:

_____

_____

QUESTION 2   1 mark

Bricklaying products are discounted by 20% in a store. If the regular retail price is $120.00, how much does the customer pay after the discount?

Answer:

_____

Measurement Conversions

QUESTION 1   1 mark

How many grams are in 1.85 kg?

Answer:

_____

_____

QUESTION 2   1 mark

How many centimetres are in 35 mm?

Answer:

_____

_____

Measurement – Area, Perimeter and Volume

Area

QUESTION 1   1 mark

The floor area of a warehouse that is being concreted measures 15 m × 6 m. What is the total floor area?

Answer:

_____

_____

QUESTION 2   1 mark

What is the total area of a driveway that measures 12.2 m × 1.5 m?

Answer:

_____

_____

Perimeter

QUESTION 1   1 mark

Calculate the perimeter of a path that is 13 m long × 3 m wide.

Answer:

_____

QUESTION 2   1 mark

Determine the perimeter of an area of a concrete slab that measures 5.4 m × 5.7 m?

Answer:

Volume

QUESTION 1   1 mark

If the floor dimensions of an equipment storage shed are 12 m × 4 m × 100 mm, how many cubic metres are there?

Answer:

QUESTION 2   1 mark

A slab for a shed has the dimensions of 11.2 m × 11.2 m × 75 mm. What is the cubic area?

Answer:

Earning Wages

QUESTION 1   1 mark

A first-year apprentice concreter gets paid $12.50 per hour. If the apprentice works for 31 hours over four days, how much is the gross pay?

Answer:

QUESTION 2   1 mark

A first-year apprentice concreter gets paid $12.50 per hour. If the apprentice works for 62 hours over an eight-day fortnight, how much is the gross pay?

Answer:

Squaring Numbers

Introducing square numbers

QUESTION 1   1 mark

What is 7^2?

Answer:

QUESTION 2   1 mark

A garage floor area measures 13 m × 13 m. What is the total floor area?

Answer:

Applying square numbers to the trade

QUESTION 1   1 mark

A patio area measures 6.4 m × 6.4 m. What is the total area, in square metres?

Answer:

QUESTION 2   1 mark

An entertainment area needs a slab poured that is 5.3 m × 5.3 m. What is the total area?

Answer:

Ratios

QUESTION 1   1 mark

The ratio to make concrete is 1 part cement, 1.5 parts sand and 3 parts aggregate.

a   If a small amount is being mixed and 1 part equals 3 kg, how many kilograms of each element are needed?

Answer:

_____

b   How many kilograms in total?

Answer:

_____

QUESTION 2   1 mark

The ratio to make concrete for foundation and footings is 1 part cement, 3 parts sand and 3 parts aggregate.

a   If a small amount is to be mixed and 1 part equals 5 kg, how many kilograms of each element are needed?

Answer:

_____

b   How many kilograms in total?

Answer:

_____

Applying Maths to the Concreting Trade

The apprentice years

QUESTION 1   2 marks

A first-year apprentice concreter gets paid $12.50 per hour. A travel allowance of $13.07 is also paid per day. If the apprentice works for 31 hours over four days, how much is earned for the working week, including allowances, before tax?

Answer:

_____

QUESTION 2   2 marks

A first-year apprentice concreter gets paid $12.50 per hour. A travel allowance of $13.07 is also paid per day. If the apprentice works for 62 hours over an eight-day fortnight, how much is earned, including allowances, before tax?

Answer:

_____

Time and motion

QUESTION 1   2 marks

A concrete finisher starts work at 7.00 a.m. and stops for a break at 9.45 a.m. for 20 minutes. Lunch is at 11.30 a.m. and is for 30 minutes. The concrete finisher then works until 2 p.m. How many hours have been worked, including breaks?

Answer:

_____

QUESTION 2   2 marks

A concrete-mixing truck driver delivers cement to a worksite. He pulls up with 6 m³ of cement and backs the truck in to pour it. He waits for eight minutes for the supervisor, who is on the phone, then takes seven minutes to set up the chute. Pouring the concrete takes him 53 minutes and cleaning the chute takes him 11 minutes.

How long does it take to complete the job? Give your answer in hours and minutes?

Answer:

_____

Interpreting tables

Thickness (mm)

Area (m²)	50	75	100	125	150
5	0.4	0.4	0.6	0.8	0.8
10	0.6	0.8	1	1.4	1.6
15	0.8	1.2	1.6	2	2.4
20	1	1.6	2	2.6	3
25	1.4	2	2.6	3.2	3.8
30	1.6	2.4	3	3.8	4.6
35	1.8	2.6	3.6	4.4	5.4
40	2	3	4	5	6
45	2.4	3.4	4.6	5.8	6.8
50	2.6	3.8	5	6.4	7.6

Use the above information to answer the following questions.

QUESTION 1   2 marks

How many cubic metres of concrete are needed for a driveway that has an area of 35 m² and a thickness of 100 mm?

Answer:

QUESTION 2   2 marks

How many cubic metres of concrete are needed for a garage floor that has an area of 45 m² and a thickness of 125 mm?

Answer:

9780170474504

Glossary

Admixture A powder or fluid that is added to concrete in order to alter or enhance its properties. An admixture might be added to a batch of concrete to slow down or speed up the setting time.

Aggregate A mixture of sand, pebbles or gravel, which is combined with a cement agent to make concrete.

Cement A mixture of crushed clay and limestone used for making mortar or concrete.

Compaction Compaction increases the strength of the concrete by removing any air bubbles and distributing the aggregates evenly throughout the mixture.

Curing Concrete must be kept damp after placement in order to reduce or slow evaporation. This process is called curing and must be undertaken to ensure that enough moisture remains present for optimum hydration.

Hydration When cement is mixed with water, a chemical reaction, called hydration, occurs that results in the creation of new compounds that fix together the aggregates within the concrete. During the hydration process, the concrete, mortar or render steadily increases in strength as the cement paste fortifies.

Lime The principal material used in mortar. Lime makes the mortar more workable and gives it a degree of flexibility, which prevents cracks due to wall movement.

Plastic shrinkage cracking Premature moisture loss from the surface of plastic concrete may cause cracking and can be attributed to hot and windy conditions.

Reinforced concrete Concrete that has steel bars, reinforcement wire or wire mesh embedded into it. Usually used for slabs and beams requiring extra strength.

Segregation An uneven distribution of both fine and coarse aggregates within the concrete. Segregation can occur if there is excess water in the mix or if the concrete has been poorly compacted. Segregation can also occur if the concrete has been poured from a height greater than two metres or if some of the cement paste has leaked from the formwork.

Water/cement ratio This term refers to the ratio of the mass of the water in the concrete in relation to the mass of the cement in the concrete, mortar, render or grout. The strength and durability of a concrete mix will be lowered when the water/cement ratio is higher.

Workability Refers to the handling, pouring and/or placing and finishing off of the concrete or mortar and how easy these processes/actions are. Generally, it is accepted that the greater the slump or water/cement ratio then the greater the workability of the concrete mix or mortar.

Formulae and Data

Area

Area = length × breadth and is given in square units
Area = l × b

Perimeter

Perimeter is the length of all sides added together.
Perimeter = length + breadth + length + breadth
Perimeter = l + b + l + b

Volume

Paths, driveways and garage floors
Volume = length × width × thickness ÷ 1000 and is given in cubic metres

Circles and triangles
Area of a circle = Pi (use $\pi = 3.14$) × radius squared × thickness ÷ 1000
Area of a triangle = $\frac{1}{2}$ × base × height × thickness ÷ 1000

Post holes

Round galvanised hollow posts into a cylindrical hole
Volume of the hole = Pi (use $\pi = 3.14$) × radius squared × depth

Rectangular timber posts into a rectangular hole
Volume of a rectangular post = width × breadth × length
Volume of a rectangular hole = 2w × 2b × depth
Volume of hole − volume of the post = cement needed

Times Tables

1

1 × 1	=	1
2 × 1	=	2
3 × 1	=	3
4 × 1	=	4
5 × 1	=	5
6 × 1	=	6
7 × 1	=	7
8 × 1	=	8
9 × 1	=	9
10 × 1	=	10
11 × 1	=	11
12 × 1	=	12

2

1 × 2	=	2
2 × 2	=	4
3 × 2	=	6
4 × 2	=	8
5 × 2	=	10
6 × 2	=	12
7 × 2	=	14
8 × 2	=	16
9 × 2	=	18
10 × 2	=	20
11 × 2	=	22
12 × 2	=	24

3

1 × 3	=	3
2 × 3	=	6
3 × 3	=	9
4 × 3	=	12
5 × 3	=	15
6 × 3	=	18
7 × 3	=	21
8 × 3	=	24
9 × 3	=	27
10 × 3	=	30
11 × 3	=	33
12 × 3	=	36

4

1 × 4	=	4
2 × 4	=	8
3 × 4	=	12
4 × 4	=	16
5 × 4	=	20
6 × 4	=	24
7 × 4	=	28
8 × 4	=	32
9 × 4	=	36
10 × 4	=	40
11 × 4	=	44
12 × 4	=	48

5

1 × 5	=	5
2 × 5	=	10
3 × 5	=	15
4 × 5	=	20
5 × 5	=	25
6 × 5	=	30
7 × 5	=	35
8 × 5	=	40
9 × 5	=	45
10 × 5	=	50
11 × 5	=	55
12 × 5	=	60

6

1 × 6	=	6
2 × 6	=	12
3 × 6	=	18
4 × 6	=	24
5 × 6	=	30
6 × 6	=	36
7 × 6	=	42
8 × 6	=	48
9 × 6	=	54
10 × 6	=	60
11 × 6	=	66
12 × 6	=	72

7

1 × 7	=	7
2 × 7	=	14
3 × 7	=	21
4 × 7	=	28
5 × 7	=	35
6 × 7	=	42
7 × 7	=	49
8 × 7	=	56
9 × 7	=	63
10 × 7	=	70
11 × 7	=	77
12 × 7	=	84

8

1 × 8	=	8
2 × 8	=	16
3 × 8	=	24
4 × 8	=	32
5 × 8	=	40
6 × 8	=	48
7 × 8	=	56
8 × 8	=	64
9 × 8	=	72
10 × 8	=	80
11 × 8	=	88
12 × 8	=	96

9

1 × 9	=	9
2 × 9	=	18
3 × 9	=	27
4 × 9	=	36
5 × 9	=	45
6 × 9	=	54
7 × 9	=	63
8 × 9	=	72
9 × 9	=	81
10 × 9	=	90
11 × 9	=	99
12 × 9	=	108

10

1 × 10	=	10
2 × 10	=	20
3 × 10	=	30
4 × 10	=	40
5 × 10	=	50
6 × 10	=	60
7 × 10	=	70
8 × 10	=	80
9 × 10	=	90
10 × 10	=	100
11 × 10	=	110
12 × 10	=	120

11

1 × 11	=	11
2 × 11	=	22
3 × 11	=	33
4 × 11	=	44
5 × 11	=	55
6 × 11	=	66
7 × 11	=	77
8 × 11	=	88
9 × 11	=	99
10 × 11	=	110
11 × 11	=	121
12 × 11	=	132

12

1 × 12	=	12
2 × 12	=	24
3 × 12	=	36
4 × 12	=	48
5 × 12	=	60
6 × 12	=	72
7 × 12	=	84
8 × 12	=	96
9 × 12	=	108
10 × 12	=	120
11 × 12	=	132
12 × 12	=	144

Multiplication Grid

	1	2	3	4	5	6	7	8	9	10	11	12
1	1	2	3	4	5	6	7	8	9	10	11	12
2	2	4	6	8	10	12	14	16	18	20	22	24
3	3	6	9	12	15	18	21	24	27	30	33	36
4	4	8	12	16	20	24	28	32	36	40	44	48
5	5	10	15	20	25	30	35	40	45	50	55	60
6	6	12	18	24	30	36	42	48	54	60	66	72
7	7	14	21	28	35	42	49	56	63	70	77	84
8	8	16	24	32	40	48	56	64	72	80	88	96
9	9	18	27	36	45	54	63	72	81	90	99	108
10	10	20	30	40	50	60	70	80	90	100	110	120
11	11	22	33	44	55	66	77	88	99	110	121	132
12	12	24	36	48	60	72	84	96	108	120	132	144

9780170474504

Notes

Notes

9780170474504

Notes

Notes

9780170474504